UNVEILING THE PHYSICAL SOURCE OF INTUITION

A Discovery that Answers What Were Thought to Be Miracles, Supernatural Phenomena, Extraordinary Events, and Coincidences

BUTHAYNA TAHA

BALBOA.PRESS
A DIVISION OF HAY HOUSE

Copyright © 2021 Buthayna Taha.

All rights reserved. No part of this book may be used or reproduced by any means, graphic, electronic, or mechanical, including photocopying, recording, taping or by any information storage retrieval system without the written permission of the author except in the case of brief quotations embodied in critical articles and reviews.

Balboa Press books may be ordered through booksellers or by contacting:

Balboa Press
A Division of Hay House
1663 Liberty Drive
Bloomington, IN 47403
www.balboapress.com
844-682-1282

Because of the dynamic nature of the Internet, any web addresses or links contained in this book may have changed since publication and may no longer be valid. The views expressed in this work are solely those of the author and do not necessarily reflect the views of the publisher, and the publisher hereby disclaims any responsibility for them.

The author of this book does not dispense medical advice or prescribe the use of any technique as a form of treatment for physical, emotional, or medical problems without the advice of a physician, either directly or indirectly. The intent of the author is only to offer information of a general nature to help you in your quest for emotional and spiritual well-being. In the event you use any of the information in this book for yourself, which is your constitutional right, the author and the publisher assume no responsibility for your actions.

Any people depicted in stock imagery provided by Getty Images are models, and such images are being used for illustrative purposes only. Certain stock imagery © Getty Images.

Print information available on the last page.

ISBN: 978-1-9822-6844-2 (sc)
ISBN: 978-1-9822-6846-6 (hc)
ISBN: 978-1-9822-6845-9 (e)

Library of Congress Control Number: 2021909209

Balboa Press rev. date: 05/28/2021

For the two precious individuals who never knew I would be a writer: my late parents, Sadik and Souad.
—One of the seeds of your eternal love, Buthayna

Acknowledgments

A book is always a product of a community, no matter what the rest out there would say. My life has been full of inspirations from within me and from the people around me: my family, my friends, and even people I barely know. While this book in particular was written with my pen, its script and flow of ideas wouldn't have evolved into this product without my allowing the impact of these inspirational people in my life to flow through the ink of my pen. As a matter of fact, it was one phone call from my youngest sister, Aisar, that started the whole thing when she said, "You have to publish your book this year. I listened to an astrologist, and she said that the year 2018 is great for publishing a book." I laughed hysterically at her request, since it didn't make any sense to me and also because it was beyond me to publish a book that fast, even though I had written most of it four years prior. So, after many conversations with her, I opened the flat white box labeled "writing" that had been idly laying atop my bedroom dresser, took out the draft of this book, and got to work, and the rest is in your hand in a paper or digital format. So thank you, my lovely sister Aisar, for that.

I have so many special people in my life for whom I'm thankful. A special thank-you to my sisters, Lamees, Nardeen, May, and Aisar;

my brother, Muthanna; my sister-in-law, Tamara; my brothers-in-law, Ali, Ammar, Jafar, and Talal; my nieces, Fatma, Zainab, Haneen, and Sarah; and my nephews, Sadik D., Mohamed, Sadik T., Ali, Ibrahim, Daud, and Salman. A genuine thank-you to a few of my dearest and best friends who encouraged me to find the time to finish this book and who tracked the progress of it with me: Alia, Maha, Nada, Nidhal, and Wafa. As for my other best friends and fabulous people in my life who didn't know much about it, I'm grateful for their presence in my life: Sydney, Kathy, Shermin, Benan, Tahrir, Barb, Beth, Haider, Karen, Mary Jo, Leisheng, Suad, Linda, Yasmin, Nakiya, Mayyada, Sally, Tanya, Annette, Jan, Carol, Marie, Becky, Arizona, Nedhal, Jannah, Ilham, Dr. Aysha, Alicia, Hana, Sahar, Hadeel, Farah, Laila, Nazli, Hajar, Helen, Dina, Asia, Laura, Ibtihaj, Hulum, Diane, Lillian, Hihumi, Dan, Isam, Janan, Pete, Mahmood, Haitham, Martin, Ahmed, Ziad, Sabah, Nikk, Hani, Don, Rashad, Carlo, Dr. Pullman, Laith, Hal, Kent, Neal, Brandon, Dr. Davidson, Raghid, Randy, Tim, Hassan, Dr. Ozog, Jeremy, Salman, Kais, Ghassan, Hamid, Aras, and Ibrahim. All of you have enriched my life, and I love you!

I'm forever thankful to Balboa Press for giving me this opportunity to self-publish my book with them. It is because of their belief that "there is a unique, independent voice in all of us just waiting to be heard" that I was encouraged to publish my book. In particular, I would like to thank senior publishing consultant Marsha Manion for her continual guidance and support during the publishing process. She called me every three weeks during the first six months to extend her support. I would also like to thank the publisher's check-in coordinator Michael March who followed up with me until the final stretch of the publishing process.

I'm here to say that none of the people I have mentioned here knew anything about this book before its publication other than its title, except for my copyeditor Jodi Brandon, for whom I'm so thankful. Her candid advice corrected lots of what I had battled with for hours. Jodi was recommended to me (thankfully) by creative writer and blogger Katie Jane Drury-Tanner, who couldn't edit my book since she was in the midst of moving to Germany with Dan and their three sons.

Contents

Prelude xv
Introduction: Why I Wrote This Book xvii

Chapter 1 What Is Intuition? 1
Chapter 2 How I Discovered the Physical Source of Intuition 3
Chapter 3 What's Your Mother Got to Do with It? 6
Chapter 4 The Physical Place of Intuition 9
Chapter 5 Why Do We Have a Sinking Feeling in the Physical Source of Intuition? 11
Chapter 6 Why Mothers Give Their Children Unconditional Love 14
Chapter 7 Flow of Intuition 17
Chapter 8 Why Do We Say Our Gut Feeling Is True? 19
Chapter 9 Trusting Your Intuition 20
Chapter 10 Human Resemblance to Trees 25
Chapter 11 Healing Power and Intuition 28
Chapter 12 The Golden Ratio and Intuition 30

Chapter 13	Human Decisions	33
Chapter 14	Your Passion and Intuition	36
Chapter 15	The Calling of Intuition	37
Chapter 16	Why Do We Channel Specific Intuitive Messages and Not Others?	40
Chapter 17	Follow Your Heart in That Moment	42
Chapter 18	We Have All the Answers	44
Chapter 19	Wanting, but Not Sure What	46
Chapter 20	Listen to the Voices of Angels, Not to the Voices of Demons	48
Chapter 21	Why Do We Say Some People Are More Loving than Others?	50
Chapter 22	How Letting Go Relates to Letting God	52
Chapter 23	How to Activate Your Intuition	53
Chapter 24	Can Intuitions Collide?	54
Chapter 25	Coincidences? I Don't Think So	55
Chapter 26	The Power of Family Prayers	57
Chapter 27	The Mystery of Identical Twins Resolved	60
Chapter 28	How Human Beings Are Connected to Each Other	61
Chapter 29	Worry, Fear, and Intuition	62
Chapter 30	Food Craving and Intuition	65
Chapter 31	The Link between Disease and Intuition	67
Chapter 32	Revenge, Anger, Hate, and Intuition	69
Chapter 33	Intuition Is to Blame for Procrastination After All	71

Chapter 34	Creativity and Intuition	75
Chapter 35	How Intuition Shaped History	76
Chapter 36	Now What?	78
Chapter 37	Intuition: Continuity and Living in the Now	79
Chapter 38	Happiness in Everything Is Connected to the Creator	80
Chapter 39	Linking Religions and Faiths Intuitionally	81
Chapter 40	How Intuitive Are You?	82

Conclusion 83

Prelude

Since I became aware of my being, I knew that, unlike any of my siblings or the people around me, I was driven by a great force that had not only shaped my life but had also led me in sneaky, unpredictable ways to where I am right now and what I'm passionately doing in my life, which is writing. Although it currently is not the only passion I have in my life, writing has been the secret companion I have had all my life. Writing has made me so comfortable expressing my journey and who I am, my wonders, my answers to great questions, and my solutions to human issues. I always say, "I don't sit down and write; I start writing and then sit down." Writing has always been spontaneous, natural, and an unplanned event for me. It is the volcano inside of me bulging out in words. I have no control or say in this matter. When I feel the urge to write, nothing can stop my stampede of thoughts. They fall one by one in front of the others while they move in my head and through my pen, just as I'm writing these thoughts right now. It doesn't matter what subject I'm writing about. The only thing that is for sure is that the passion of the words and ideas ironically comes from my intuition and from my deep desire to share my feelings and my ideas with the world.

I feel that the universe beats in me. And that is why I deeply belong to what I've written and suggest in this book. I don't think that if I believed otherwise I would have been chosen to live this life in particular. I'm confident that I'm not the only one who feels that way.

Introduction
Why I Wrote This Book

I have always tried to fathom the source of human intuition in general. But my intuition, which led me to write about intuition itself, originated from a deep desire within me that grew more intense the more I wanted to know the basis for trusting my intuitive self. Because I'm so intense most of the time, my intuitive self has always been decisive regarding how I make my choices, why I am here and not somewhere else, and why I am writing this book and not a different one. Consequently, I wanted to know more about it in order to trust this thrust of undeniable information and guidance. I wanted to fully trust it so I could surrender to it totally instead of resisting what had been coming to me. I know this is true for so many of you, if not all of you. Otherwise, you wouldn't be reading this book. But my quest for intuition led me to a more mysterious question that caused my brain to ache for so long: Where is intuition in my body—its physical place of origin? The journey of my thoughts and contemplations, while giving full throttle to my intuition itself, grew more fascinating and intriguing as I continued to write. All of a sudden, it took only one moment of thought for me to discover the physical source of intuition. The entire logic of it manifested in my mind in a flash, as if it were an episode of déjà vu.

But you don't need to worry. I will let you travel with me through my journey of this discovery. I'll provide evidences of it and support it, chapter after chapter. What's intriguing is not the discovery itself but rather the evidence that supports it. I promise that after you finish reading, you will have answers to so many questions you have related to spirituality in general and intuition in particular. I am, in fact, writing this book on behalf of all of you. These words and discussions are not mine. They are available information in our universe. And I'm just the one who was chosen to tune into them, channel them, and convey them to the rest of you, just as my spiritual teacher in life, American self-help author and motivational speaker Dr. Wayne W. Dyer (may his soul rest in peace) used to say in his talks and writings. It came to me the same way. Here I would like to confidently state that the content and findings I describe in this book are not based on any religious belief, spiritual practice, ethnic affiliation, or race group. They are unbiased, universal, and spiritual, and they have no specific identity. And in an effort not to offend your beliefs, whatever they are, and to make you comfortable during this conversation, I am going to refer to the source of all beings in the universe, or what we call cosmic consciousness—the source of everything—as the Creator, the Source, and God, alternately.

1
What Is Intuition?

Intuition is an undeniable urge to feel or do something. Maybe one morning you feel strongly that you should not take the freeway to go to work, or for no logical reason you feel you need to stop by your mother's house. When you feel strongly about something without knowing why, intuition is in play. It's like relying on something beyond yourself. Intuition, in my opinion, is the highest dimension of our existence. It is the whisper of our souls inside of us. It repeats specific powerful messages all the time, but it is not to be mistakenly identified as schizophrenia. Intuition always gives us hints and steers us back to the same ideas and urges. And when our minds and logic dismiss these whispers with solid reasons, it doesn't take that much time for them to appear again, asking us to fulfill them. It reminds me of a kid who nags his or her parents for something, only for the parents to dismiss the kid. But then the kid persists until the parents give up and take the time to look into the kid's demand.

While I was pondering the energy fields of the human body (since I have no doubt in my mind, and I'm sure you don't either, that intuition is nothing more than energy), I came across an interesting article by Phylameana Lila Desy, "Five Layers of the Human Energy Field." Learn Religions, Aug. 26, 2020, https://www.learnreligions.com/layers-of-human-energy-field-1729677. In this article, she wrote about the five layers of the human energy fields. From the closest to the physical human body outward, they are physical energy, etheric energy, emotional energy, mental energy, and spiritual energy. Desy described the final layer, the spiritual energy, as where our consciousness, which we also call "higher awareness," resides. How this finding relates to where in the human body intuition resides will be revealed in coming chapters. You will see how fascinating it is, and no other energy field can be associated with it.

Intuition is this significant layer of our energy where the soul engages in a conversation with the ego and taps into it, if you will.

As human beings, we have a few of what I call "spiritual energy organs," which differ from physical organs not only because they are energy and not physically visible but also because they differ in the manner of their growth. They do not need nutrients, and they don't follow the aging process. Rather, their growth rates depend on an individual's conscious and subconscious enrichments. In addition, unlike with physical organs, there is no limit to their growth and fulfillment. But I want to be clear here: all of these energy organs are connected with physical organs and ultimately mold us into the mind/body/soul entities that we are.

One of these fascinating energy organs is intuition itself. And while you might conclude as of now that it is unidentifiable, this book will connect it to our physicality and point to the physical source of intuition.

2

How I Discovered the Physical Source of Intuition

The Journey of Discovering the Physical Source of Intuition

On April 19, 2010, a week after an intense conversation about spirituality with some friends regarding our diverse inherited religious beliefs, I had an epiphany that gave me chills and transformed my spiritual journey. I realized an incredible fact about myself: the only thing I have been fully trusting unconsciously in my life is my intuition. My intuition was tested on the day I discovered the rationale behind my position on the most crucial choice I had ever been challenged with. If my intuition had convinced me, for example, to convert to the specific religion we were discussing, which requires practicing rituals and adhering to teachings in order not to go to hell, I would have done it, since I fear punitive suffering as eternal punishment so much. But I didn't feel that, because the voice in the core of my being, which I always refer to as my intuition, has no doubt that it knows the real truth, and that is why it is superior to the idea (without a trace of doubt) that I will go to hell if I don't follow that specific religion. My intuition is where I test the truth about anything in life. This conclusion immediately became a fact that was carved in my being and will be for the rest of my life.

After confidently believing that my intuition has the ultimate source of truth, I started to dwell on the questions that kept me awake many nights: Where does the source of the truth—the whole truth—reside in this universe? And which entity has full possession and ownership of this abundant and limitless information? Where does it come from? I woke up one night, sat up in my bed with a racing heartbeat and shortness of breath, kept my eyes closed, and said to myself, "Wait a minute. Isn't that the ultimate quest of every human being on this earth—the quest for the supreme entity, the omnipotent entity who creates and possesses everything?" The answer was ineluctable, predetermined, and inevitable: "Of course; it is the Creator of the universe." Then, with a slower heartbeat and deeper breaths, I could hear myself whispering again. "Of course. Of course it is. Who else is limitless and has abundance of everything in this universe, including the truth?

What I'm concluding here is that if my intuition has the truth and if the source of truth is the Creator, then my intuition is linked directly to the Creator. If so, then how, where, and why is that possible? And if my intuition is where I test the truth about anything in my life, and if the truth is residing in me, then how is it possible that I'm tapping into it?

Intuition is the only connection we have to the Creator, the Source, God, or whatever you want to call this entity. It candidly displays the truth about us in everything in order for us to follow it. That is why when we don't follow it, we feel horrible and not like ourselves, as if we are going against who we really are. So who we are is manifested and guided by intuition. And that thing in us we call intuition, which is wired to the Creator, has the truth. It is authentic. And this is what we should trust.

Now that we have established that intuition's truth is connected to the Creator, this leads to the most intriguing question of this book: Where in our beings are we physically connected to the Creator? Where could this connection or receptor be in our bodies? Keep this question in the back of your mind while I discuss the next fascinating clue in my quest of finding the physical source of intuition. I won't keep you wondering long about the answers and my discovery. As a matter of fact, you will know it in the coming chapters, as I want to follow up with my discovery chapter after chapter, supporting and affirming my claims. The real suspense of this book is not the discovery itself but rather how the discovery is going to make all aspects of our spiritual and nonspiritual practices make sense and give answers to what were long thought to be miracles, supernatural phenomena, extraordinary coincidences, and unusual and surprising events. This book discusses all of them.

3

What's Your Mother Got to Do with It?

The First Evidence of the Physical Place of Intuition

The answer to where our intuition is physically connected to the Creator and this abundance of information is quite simple and evident. It is where the Creator left us on this earth. Yes, it is our mother indeed. But how and exactly where would that be? I mentioned in the introduction that it took a moment's thought for me to discover the physical source of intuition. Here is how it unfolded in my brain.

My theory about the physical source of intuition is best described by first mentioning the sinking feeling in our stomachs that we all feel once in a while. (I describe this in more detail in chapter 4.) The sinking feeling has a physical place that goes into our stomachs. Why does it go there in particular and not somewhere else in our bodies, such as our chests or our heads? It does so simply because God's connection to us resides right there. How is that possible?

In the womb (the uterus) during pregnancy, the fetus's stomach is attached to the mother's placenta by the umbilical cord; it is the source of life. The placenta itself, which is attached to the wall of the mother's uterus, is a temporary organ that joins mother and fetus. It is a mass of blood vessels that transport oxygen and nutrients from the mother's blood to the fetus and permits the release of carbon dioxide and waste products from the fetus.

After birth, the umbilical cord is cut to detach the newborn from the mother. What's left of the umbilical cord becomes useless, and the newborn's body closes the area and creates what is called the umbilicus. Traces and remains of the umbilical cord reside just behind the belly button, or what is medically called the navel. In other words, the umbilicus, which is in the navel area, is the scarred place where the umbilical cord was attached to the fetus's abdomen; it is usually called the "umbilical cord remnant." This tissue supported the umbilical cord during pregnancy. It is where we were disconnected from our mothers after we were connected to God, the Creator, thus making it the physical place of our creation and the answer to our question of where the Creator left us on this earth. And the sinking feeling I was just talking about relates to our last physical connection with God, which is that area. The entity that exists between a mother and her child since conception is God. (I'll carry all that I've talked about so far into the following chapters to explain how and why these are facts.)

A unique connection exists, therefore, between God and the womb. Through the womb, we get a glimpse of the Almighty's qualities and attributes. The umbilicus nurtures, feeds, and shelters us in the early stages of life.

My spiritual conclusion is that in a mother's womb, the umbilical cord is the source of life. When it is cut after childbirth, the disconnection is replaced by the Creator's energy as a permanent connection of the child to the universe via the umbilical cord remnant.

When we are cut from our mother's cord, the only nourishment we are left with is God's, which is unlimited, eternal, and abundant. It is up to us to open our hearts to it and tap into it. It is no miracle that we live so long, experience so much, and still survive. God gives us this great power, which gives us continuity and sustains us. And it is this connection that keeps us connected to the unlimited abundant source of information that intuition is part of.

4

The Physical Place of Intuition

Surely you have had a sinking feeling in your stomach and wondered why. My theory is that the stomach is where our feelings and emotions literally sink to their originating place: the Source, or God. I do think that sinking feeling goes there to escape the feeling of human ego and goes to its source. But why does it do this? It does so because it seeks the unconditional love that will protect it. After all, this is where life started, as discussed in the previous chapter. Life moved from God to the placenta to the umbilical cord remnants behind the belly button. This is where it will end, too. I'm suggesting this will happen in a literal way. Physical life ends when the soul departs the body and exits from the belly button to reunite once again with its Source.

Since the umbilical cord remnant is the physical place of our creation and where the Creator left us on this earth, as was concluded in the previous chapter, mothers are the vessels of the Creator's plugs, transporting them permanently into our bodies. As a matter of fact, these plugs are energy fields that encapsulate the remnant of our last connection with the Creator—the remnant of the umbilical cord behind the belly button.

We all walk with such plugs in our bodies, so to speak; they originate from the area of umbilical cord residues and extend outside our bodies. These fascinating plugs connect us to our Source. Each of us protects it since conception; in the womb, the fetal position covers it, protecting it from harm, and we continue doing protecting it during our lives. Whenever we want to protect ourselves, we wrap our hands around our bellies while tilting our heads toward our belly buttons. We subconsciously realize the umbilical remnant's sacredness, its uniqueness, and its vital importance to our survival.

Since there is no such thing as solid material and everything is energy, this plug is a realm of a concentrated energy field that is host to so many things, including intuition, making the plug one of the energy organs I mentioned in Chapter 1. It is in turn molded with the physical body in the umbilical cord remnant, marking it as the physical source and place of intuition in our bodies.

5

Why Do We Have a Sinking Feeling in the Physical Source of Intuition?

As explained previously, the sinking feeling in our stomachs when we are feeling scared, anxious, or nervous is experienced exactly underneath our belly button area, in the residual mass of the umbilical cord. That sinking feeling is not purely a fight-or-flight response from our amygdala. My theory is that it is a spasm within that area emanating from our Source—from our connection to the universe—which is so vulnerable and sensitive to the measure of love. The sinking feeling is activated in a spasm when love, which is always a high energy, is lowered by low-energy feelings of uncomfortable fear, hate, anxiousness, or nervousness.

You get this feeling in your stomach because your essential self—your soul—wants to communicate with its Creator. When this area is energized, it plugs itself into the Source and gives us what we call a sinking feeling.

Subconsciously, you always get information from the outside world via this plug. And before you do anything with it, the information goes immediately through your belly button down to the Source connection to have its authenticity evaluated, since intuition is where truth resides. And if it is aligned with your energy and vibration, and with the Source, you will feel *good* about it without knowing why. And the opposite happens when the information is not aligned with the Source: you feel *bad* or uncomfortable without knowing why. That interactive communication is referred to as "intuition."

This sinking feeling typically does not last more than a few seconds, because when the mind realizes and seizes it, it starts connecting the mind to that feeling and tries to make a connection with logic rather than intuition. These few seconds emanate from the source of intuition, the consciousness, which is separate from the mind. When you put the mind into action, it starts the logic of analyzing, and subsequently it loses its connection to the abundant source of information—the Creator. Thus, intuition is lost. This is why we sometimes feel that we are so close in thoughts to who we are or what our mission in life is during what I call "intuitive flares." These thoughts slip away as soon as our minds interfere, and we lose the connection to the abundance of information. Again, this proves that the one that hijacks and interrupts an intuitive flare is the mind.

Any unaligned feeling or encounter of a frequency different from that of the Creator will cause a sinking feeling and butterflies in one's stomach. This includes fear of anything, anxiety, and bad decisions. When you feel depressed, you have a sinking feeling. Why? Because time is not a factor here. Therefore, intuition does not align with this fact and rebels against it. This causes a sinking feeling. The sinking feeling signals unalignment with the Source. It's a signal that something bad is happening.

The Sinking Feeling and Derailment

When you do (or just think about) something that's not true to your intuition and not within your path, that derailment causes your essential self to be distant from its Source. It cannot identify itself with the Source. It loses some of its identity, and that by itself makes the essential self give a command to its physical being. The umbilical cord remains, and this negative energy, or derailment, is transmitted to the physical place of the soul and will cause a spasm type of feeling—the sinking feeling. Any feeling or frequency that is unaligned with the Source will cause a sinking feeling.

Another theory about the sinking feeling is that the frequency of love is the highest and the frequency of fear is the lowest. Since your plug with the Source is of a higher frequency, resembling God's frequency, and since the information going to the plug from your exterior energy is of a low frequency, when they clash, a squeeze of energy happens. That squeeze is what we call a sinking feeling.

6

Why Mothers Give Their Children Unconditional Love

Love is the most positive energy anyone can transmit to others. It is comforting, therapeutic, healing, and the most powerful thing in this universe.

A mother's love for her child is one of the most mysterious phenomena in human relations. Almost all mothers give their children unconditional love. (I say "almost" to exclude those who painfully have mental illnesses that often affect their actions in society, especially with the people they should love the most—their children.)

A mother carries her baby, a piece of the Creator, during pregnancy, giving continuity to life because the link between a mother and a child is established by the Creator—the pure love—via the umbilical cord. Continuation and flow of the Creator goes from the mother via the umbilical cord to the child.

Since the physical source of our intuition is the traces of the umbilical cord, and since the umbilical cord is from our mother, then her unconditional love for us is transmitted to us from her via the umbilical cord. And the reason mothers give us a love that is unconditional is because they give us life via umbilical cords, which is descended from God as pure unconditional love from God.

After we are born, that love stays with us at the umbilical cord remnant. Since the umbilical cord is the source of life because of its connection to the Source, and since its umbilicus (its remnant) is where intuition is ultimately molded in our physical bodies as mentioned previously, *intuition is an energy of pure love.*

Why don't children have same unconditional love for their mothers that their mothers have for them? Physics undoubtedly can answer this question. Blood and God flow in one direction: *from* the mother *to* the child. Thus, the mother is the supplier and the child is the receiver.

The Second Law of Thermodynamics

The second law of thermodynamics tells us that energy always moves from a more concentrated (high quality) condition to a less concentrated (low quality) one http://www.ftexploring.com/energy/2nd Law-P2.html. Thus, energy gets diluted. The movement will stop when there is no longer a difference in concentration, meaning the system is in equilibrium. Since the Source's energy and love are endless, the equilibrium in this case will never happen, and God's energy, love, and abundance information will flow through the mother and from the mother to the child, and will continue for eternity. You might ask how the flow continues after birth. That's the whole notion of this book: that the residue of the umbilical cord will keep plugging us to the nonphysical source of creation through its antenna. Therefore, we are never separated from the Creator. We are always remotely connected to the source of creation through its energy antenna plug. Think about that and allow it to marinate in your thoughts while you continue to read this book.

God grants human beings the most precious gift of all: His love. God's love is transported from Him to humans through mothers' placentas. As I just suggested, energy flows from the most concentrated to the least concentrated. Because of the Creator's abundant infinite love, it will take an infinite amount of time for this equilibrium of love to happen—that is, the leveling of love between God and human. That is why love flows in one direction: from God to mother to child. It will never end, and it will never reverse direction.

Does the child have unconditional love for his mother, the same as she has for her child? Yes and no. The answer is yes when the child is still in the mother's womb and still attached to the placenta. The baby in the womb is pure love because he is fully attached to God, who is represented here by the placenta. And the answer is no immediately after the umbilical cord is cut from the placenta, at which point the baby is no longer fully attached to the placenta, the source of absolute pure love. The answer is no also because divine love—unconditional love—is one-way, as just described. It flows from the source of God, the placenta, to the baby according to the second law of thermodynamics. Energy flows from the more concentrated condition to the less concentrated one.

7

Flow of Intuition

Based on the findings in chapter 6, we know the flow of the abundance of limitless information that has the truth, which flows to our intuition plug, is also governed by the second law of thermodynamics, which explains how energy flows from more concentrated to less concentrated areas. This is because the Source has abundance and endless information, thus making intuition keep moving in one direction, as per this simplified flow sequence I suggest here:

The Creator (source of life and of limitless, abundance information)

--->

Miracle of Conception (through the mother)

--->

Umbilical Cord (attaching the mother's placenta to the fetus during pregnancy)

--->

Umbilicus (the Creator's plug in our bodies; the umbilical cord remnant after fetus detachment from the mother)

--->

Intuition (energy organ; abundant, readily available information that emanates from the Creator's plug/antenna receptor in the umbilicus, which is wired to God and where truth and love reside)

As noted in chapter 1, spiritual energy is where the consciousness, or what we also call "higher awareness," resides. And since this energy field is the furthest energy layer to our bodies, and the one that encompasses all other energies around our bodies, this is where the final attachment of the plug of the antenna to the Source shall be, therefore making the spiritual energy what is attached to the physical source of intuition in our bodies: the umbilical cord remnant behind the navel.

8

Why Do We Say Our Gut Feeling Is True?

This statement is powerful. Again, the gut feeling, which resides in the placenta's umbilical cord, remains our plug and connection to our Source—to God. Gut feeling emanates from a source of unconditional love, abundance, information, eternal existence, and the source of ultimate truth, which is the Creator—the only entity who has the truth, as explained in earlier chapters. Thus, this makes the gut feeling always true.

9

Trusting Your Intuition

Why—and How—to Trust the Thrust of Intuition

> Every right decision I've made - every *right* decision I've ever made - has come from my gut.
> —Oprah Winfrey (June 15, 2008, Stanford University commencement speech)

Let's pause to think about the decisions we've already made in our lives. To simplify this process, write down the decisions that have been most important in your life. For me, I'm amazed and intrigued to say without a trace of exaggeration that 100 percent of the milestone decisions I have made throughout my life that were based on my pure intuition only have been the best decisions I've ever made. As for the decisions I made while overlooking what my intuition suggested when making them, and when basing them on my logic, my feeling of right or wrong, what people around me thought was best for the situation, or the fear that overwhelmed them, I've been paying the price for them every day—not in the form of regrets, since I'm past blames and regrets, but rather in living a life of difficulties. These decisions do not match what have become of me or my lifestyle, since they were not perfect decisions when made. Yes, they might have served the moments perfectly then, but they were never the right decisions—never. This fact about my decision-making mechanism was one of the drivers that made me explore and ultimately write this book.

Sometimes when we have to make decisions, we find ourselves unsure, doubtful, confused, and frustrated, especially when time is pressing. One minute we are leaning toward one thing, and the next minute we are leaning toward its extreme in action and principle. The decision made based on pure intuition is what our pure souls and destined paths want for us, yet the other, in comparison, is based on fear and judgment of others orchestrated in our minds in a solid and brilliant way, not to be denied. That is why most human decisions are the latter, since they are the easiest and falsely considered the safest, yet not perfect. It's as if we are programmed to trust and pursue what our minds are telling us more than our intuition.

I just offered both my proof and conclusion from my personal experience as to why you need to trust your thrust of intuition when making any decision. What does "trusting your intuition" mean in this context? When your guts tell you without a doubt to do something, trust them in that moment. In the future, you will know that it was 100 percent right to do so. While your logic, your brain, and social pressure around you might be telling you otherwise, just trust in the *thrust* of your intuition at any given moment, and don't let fear or society dictate your decisions and ultimately your destined path, which you own as a creature in this universe.

The undeniable question here, though, is this: Is it rational to trust your intuition? I honestly don't know how to rationalize it and convince you of it. But I guarantee you that the more you trust yourself to make decisions based on intuition, the more it becomes a rational way for you to do so. Ironically, you just need to trust in yourself and believe that you are making the right decision.

Neuroscientist Valerie Van Mulukom, a research fellow of psychology at Coventry University in England, explained this question in her article "Is it Rational to Trust Your Gut Feelings? A Neuroscientist Explains", May 16, 2018, https://theconversation.com/is-it-rational-to-trust-your-gut-feelings-a-neuroscientist-explains-95086. She explained that intuition is the result of a fast process in the brain and continued to talk about how relying on intuition had a bad reputation, especially when making important decisions that ought to be thought of rationally. She explained that it is a myth of the cognitive process to think that intuition is a dumb response that needs to be ignored or be corrected by rational faculties. That intuition is indeed a form of information processing that is automatic and subconscious, unlike analytic thinking, which is logical and intellectual. I'm fascinated by her saying that intuition occurs when the brain makes a match or mismatch between a cognitive model and current experience before reaching the conscious awareness, and that overthinking hinders the decision-making process.

Pure intuition, for me, overrides any analytic thinking process. I think intuition is beyond our brains.

The other important question, or even dilemma, for us is how to distinguish between the true voice of our intuition and all the voices we should not listen to. I like the process and its sequence discussed by Zoe Quiney in the article "Listen to Your Heart: 7 Ways to Trust Your Intuition", March 21, 2014, https://www.rebellesociety.com/2014/03/21/2014-03-21-listen-to-your-heart-7-ways-to-trust-your-intuition/. Here's what I think about the seven ways she touched on:

1. **Just breathe.** This affirms my theory about connecting to the Source and tapping into information and truth. Breathing facilitates connecting us to the universe and the Source. And taking a deep breath many times affirms to us whether whatever we feel deep inside is what we should trust and act upon.

2. **Trust in yourself.** You are the only one who is connected to it—not anyone else. If you want to be true to yourself and your path, always trust your intuition and follow it, despite what other people suggest to you. They are not you. You are the only one who is *you*.

3. **Look for signs.** When what we call coincidences happen and happen more often, there is a message from the universe trying to affirm something to us and to give us signs to trust the emerging feeling and thrust to pursue doing something.

4. **Let go and smile.** We should not beat ourselves up all our lives for decisions that end up not to our liking later in life. Everything happens for a reason.

5. **Trust that the universe wants the best for you.** This is so true, as most of us know very well. As a matter of fact, if you swim against the flow of the river of life, you will suffer and might never see the rest of your path. We should just enjoy the ride and the journey—its uncertainty and moments of new discoveries of ourselves and the world around us.

6. **Just move.** Since the earth moves, our blood moves; we need to move physically and mentally. All things—events, the universe, people, and time—are all moving. That is

how we grab the opportunities we want as we go and grab the decisions that pop up during this journey.

7. **And create.** As I explain in more detail in chapter 34, creativity is a result of letting go and letting the God in you create.

Whatever dominates your thoughts on a regular basis has been initiated and reflected from your intuition, and it will end up being your destined path. That's the power of your intuition. One of my favorite sayings is "To unlock your destined path, you have to be open to all possibilities." And your intuition is your best source of information and possibilities. You have the power to change anything in your life by tuning into yourself and listening to what it asks of and says to you.

Here is one of the most powerful affirmations from Buddha himself: "Listen to your inner voice of reason (your conscience, intuition, holy spirit). If you don't listen to it, it slowly weakens, until you can no longer hear it … if you seriously can't hear it, then it seems you have killed or muted the voice within."

Another famous voice who spoke passionately and undeniably about listening to gut intuition while dismissing science and logic was Albert Einstein, who said, "I believe in intuitions and inspirations … I sometimes feel that I am right. I do not know that I am" (from an interview with G. S. Viereck titled "What Life Means to Einstein," which appeared in the *Saturday Evening Post* on October 26, 1929).

10
Human Resemblance to Trees

As a visual person, I understand things only when I imagine them, visualize them, or even draw them. In an effort to understand the human placenta, I started to sketch it in different forms. The resemblance of the placenta to a tree became so obvious to me. (See figure 1.) No better metaphor came to my mind, resembling the flow of life in any living thing, than that of a tree. The human placenta looks like tree roots transporting food to the tree from the ground (earth). In the case of the human placenta, though, it is transporting food to the fetus from the mother. Here are my modest equations:

Mother (A) = earth (AA)
Placenta (B) = tree root (BB)
Umbilical cord (C) = tree trunk (CC)
Baby (D) = branches/leaves/flowers (DD)

In the case of the tree, its roots anchor it to earth and extract food and moisture from earth. The root is integrated with Mother

Earth. Similarly, in the case of the fetus, the placenta anchors to the mother's womb and gets food and oxygen. The placenta is integrated with the mother, as shown in figure 1.

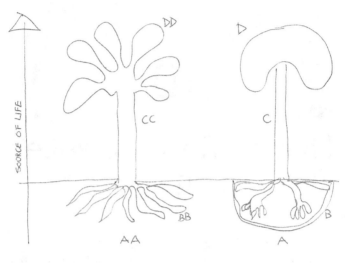

Figure 1

Navel

Let's dive into some science, some fiction, and some fun facts about the navel area, or what we call the umbilical cord remnant.

What Chinese medicine says about the navel area, its significance, and its connection to healing affirms my theory regarding the physical place of intuition. In her book *The Art Of Palpatory Diagnosis in Oriental Medicine*, published by Harcourt Publishers in London, England, in 2001, Dr. Skya Abbate, a Doctor of Oriental Medicine and Doctor of Bioethics, says that according to Chinese acupuncture, acupuncture point CV 8 Shen Que (Spirit Gate) is, in fact, the place where humans received life from their mothers by way of the umbilical cord. It is the center of energy in our bodies where our spiritual, mental, emotional, and physical health originate and reside, and it is called the "Hara" in Japanese and "Lower Dantian" in Chinese. It is where life was given to us, is sustained, and will ultimately be taken away from us.

Dr. Abbate also says that yoga, belly dancing, breathing exercises, and meditations have considered the abdomen as the center of energy that regulates the blood of the entire physical body. That is why acupuncture point CV 8 Shen Que is able to treat hundreds of diseases: it regulates the nervous, hormonal, and immune systems and, in turn, heals the organs.

At the end of the article, Dr. Abbate touches on what the Nanjing believes regarding the navel region being the center of heaven that is ruled by earth and the five element correspondences (the spleen, the stomach, the lungs, and the kidneys) to Chinese acupuncture. In short, as Yoshimaso Todo, founder of modern-day Japanese acupuncture, affirms in the same article, the abdomen is the source of life, and that is the reason why most diseases are rooted in it.

From a more spiritual context, Vithal Nadkarni, a senior consultant with the Times of India group, published an article online called "The Navel's Key Significance" (on May 24, 2006), in which he shares some of the significances of the navel. He says that St. Thomas Aquinas considered the navel to be the metaphor for spiritual things in the body. He also talks about navel gazing, which is considered one of the most profound human activities, in which individuals try to find their spiritualty in the centers of their bodies. Then he talks about how the navel is considered the center of the vital breath and balance point during the practice of yoga. Nadkarni also says that Sigmund Freud believed that dream interpretation could be located in the navel because of its psychic significance. That indeed adds another valued opinion to the importance of the navel area.

11

Healing Power and Intuition

In April 2011, I accidentally discovered a kind of healing power inside of me. I put it into use, and it worked. As I continue to practice it, I've found that it not only heals ailments, illnesses, and diseases, but also that it answers, accomplishes, or makes come true the specific intended wishes and prayers. (I perform these actions while opening this healing power from within.) I am not a healing practitioner; I just do this when I feel my intuition is tapping into it and when the person needing it asks for it and truly believes in it.

In chapter 26, I touch more on how the healing mechanism evolves. It is no coincidence that when I discovered the source and place of intuition in our bodies, which is what this book is all about, I immediately knew the physical place where my healing power originates. It is the second affirmation that both intuition and healing emanate from the same place of abundance and limitless energy and information. When I tap into the channeling of God's power through me to get the healing flow within me and outside of me, I feel it is generated from my stomach, where the residue of the umbilical cord resides in me.

This made me link the umbilical cord to the flow of source of the Creator within me. That is why I subconsciously feel heat in my belly button when I concentrate on receiving a healing energy. Why heat? This, of course, has a lot to do with the fact that the more one is connected to the Source, the more vibrations (high frequency, energized) one will feel in the "plug" described in previous chapters. These concentrated vibrations will generate high-frequency energy transmitted as heat.

12

The Golden Ratio and Intuition

The golden ratio is represented by the Greek letter ϕ (phi) and is simply the mathematical figure 1.618. It is derived from the expression a + b/a = a/b = 1.618. Also called the divine section or golden proportion, the golden ratio was termed the "Divine Proportion" by Italian mathematician Luca Pacioli in his body of work *De Divina Proportione,* published in 1509. This work explored the mathematics of the golden ratio and how it creates pleasing and harmonious proportions, which fascinated and was implemented by artists, architects, and scientists alike throughout history. As a matter of fact, Roman author and architect Vitruvius was the first to discuss the perfect proportion in architecture and the human body in his work *De Arcitectura,* written between 30 BC and 15 BC. This work, in turn, inspired Leonardo Da Vinci to draw the encoded human proportion *The Vitruvian Man* around 1490. Basically, *The Vitruvian Man*'s basic suggestion is that the human body has proportions approximately equal to that golden ratio. (See figure 2.)

Unveiling the Physical Source of Intuition

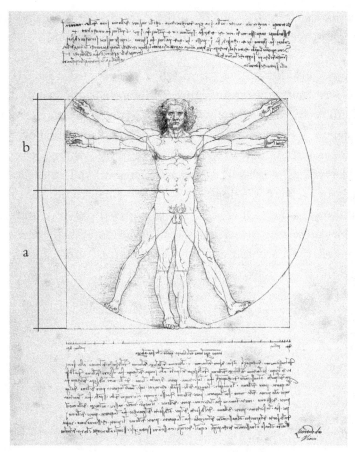

Figure 2: Vitruvian Man painted by
Leonardo da Vinci from 1492

The golden ratio has been used for centuries in architecture. But do you think there is another reason besides it being aesthetically pleasing? I wouldn't ask this rhetorical question if the answer was no. How does *The Vitruvian Man* relate to the physical source of intuition in our bodies? It has everything to do with it. As a matter of fact, it beautifully affirms my theory and discovery of the one and only physical source of intuition in our body. First, the fact that the focal point of the golden ratio of *The Vitruvian Man* is the navel itself says a great deal about its importance.

Second, the measurement from the navel to the floor and from the top of the head to the navel is the golden ratio itself.

I suggest another finding through *The Vitruvian Man*. As *The Vitruvian Man* shows us in figure 2, the navel is the center of the human body and ultimately the center of the whole universe. It is the center of the human body's connection to the world beyond its realm, and inside within its eternal power. It is where the human body revolves, connects, is centered, creates, and ends. See the circles of life in it. We don't know if they emanate from the navel or go toward them. It is both, as life throbs through us and from us. The universe is a reflection of us. We undoubtedly create the universe, the consciousness, the experiences, the realities, our lives, and ultimately our demises.

13

Human Decisions

(And Why You Should Not Act upon Thoughts when You Are in Doubt)

Humans have a tendency when making decisions to be guided by exterior forces without paying attention to the most trusted one: human intuition. Is this by virtue of how we are raised or what, ironically speaking, our intuition tells us to do?

If you are in doubt about doing something, taking an action of some sort, or going somewhere, these actions have already been examined by your intuition and the source of information. Because whatever it is does not align totally with what the Source intends in the moment and with what might happen afterward, your intuition is guiding you and giving you the best clue, which is not to proceed, in a form of what we call "doubt." So when you feel that, just don't do whatever you are in doubt about doing. It is not the right time to do it or pursue it. Maybe do it the next day or at another future time when you don't have such a doubt about doing or pursuing the activity. Your intuition is giving you the go-ahead. Everything is aligned for such actions.

But how do you know that you are truly aligned with your intuition and that you are not somehow derailed? Well, you will know. It will feel great. You will feel so connected and true to yourself. You will feel the flashes of love, light, and energy that give you the feeling that you can do anything and that nothing is impossible and nothing can stop you. On the contrary, you will feel hesitation, fear, discomfort, and agitation if you are not aligned in your thought and action to your intuition. But what if you don't have these two extremes? What if you are in between and don't know what to do? What if there's no clear answer in sight? Wait it out, contemplate, meditate, and then wait for the signs the universe will hint to you. In other words, wait for clarity. Wait until the dust—the fog—settles, as you should do in all matters in life. Then you will know without any doubt which direction you are leaning toward. You will know the path you need to take. The mist and the clouds of unclarity will dissipate. You will truly feel great to have waited for such a resolve. This, however, might take minutes, hours, days, or even months.

Ancient Chinese philosopher and writer Lao Tzu alluded to this in his book about the source and ideal of all existence, *Tao Te Ching*, https://www.goodreads.com/quotes/341604-do-you-have-the-patience-to-wait-till-your-mud, accessed April 8, 2019, in which he wrote, "Do you have the patience to wait till your mud settles and the water is clear? Can you remain unmoving till the right action arises by itself?"

I have almost never been fond of making long-term plans, especially for vacations. I have always wondered about that, since I see my friends doing so, planning months or even years in advance for vacations or reunions. While writing this book, and because of the way this book was written (that is, through spontaneous thoughts and discoveries), I discovered why I've never liked to plan ahead; it is because I have always been governed by my intuition. And since intuition is a "now" sensation, then how can I know what the "now" of next month or one year from now shall be? Intuition is unpredictable. That is why it is fascinating. The only way to know what your intuition tells you is "now."

This intuition-based behavior is valid for almost everything, from grocery shopping, visiting or calling friends, and watching movies, to more crucial decisions, such as deciding on a career, making decisions related to personal life, and so forth.

Why do people override their intuition to do or not do things? This is a big and diverse subject, but in short it is because they are scared to pursue what their intuitions are telling them to do, especially when they are not logical or when people are just trying to live in a survival mode and don't want to take a chance on this gut feeling.

14

Your Passion and Intuition

We have been discussing the quick decisions we make in our lives and their connection to intuition. But what about the passions we were born with? What does intuition have to do with them? Dr. Wayne Dyer wrote on his blog, "Your Passionate Power", accessed January 21, 2018, https://www.drwaynedyer.com/blog/tag/no-excuses/. Here is some of what he said: "The presence of passion within you is the greatest gift you can receive. And when it's aligned with Spirit, treat it as a miracle, doing everything you can to hold on to it. I feel this way about the creation of my books."

Didn't you feel speechless after reading that? I did! What Dr. Dyer said summed it all up regarding the passion we are born with—the pure calling. This passion is a permanent solid thing in our intuition. It is our pure connection to the Source, or God. This is the perfect time to discuss an intriguing finding regarding what constitutes the DNA of your passion and calling in life, which I do in the next chapter.

15

The Calling of Intuition

We are all born with internal eyes that see our callings in life. So many things happen in our lives, but why do only specific things stick out in our lives and memories, and not others? What appeals to you and gets your attention has been attracted to your "calling of intuition" by your soul-type category. For those who believe in reincarnation, soul types do not change throughout all lifetimes. According to Michael Teachings, there are seven types of human souls: the Server soul, the Artisan soul, the Worrier soul, the Scholar soul, the Sage soul, the Priest soul, and the King soul (http://personalityspirituality.net/2010/06/23/the-seven-soul-types-what-do-they-look-like/). Here are their typical traits:

- Servers: accommodating, caring, modest, dedicated, downtrodden
- Artisans: inventive, imaginative, innovative, idiosyncratic, flaky
- Warriors: forceful, assertive, feisty, determined, ruthless, vicious

- Scholars: curious, knowledgeable, analytical, dry, detached, aloof
- Sages: expressive, eloquent, witty, entertaining, flamboyant, loud
- Priests: fervent, visionary, hope-inspiring, preachy, fanatical
- Kings: commanding, masterful, self-assured, decisive, intolerant

If you were born with an Artisan soul, for example, that's what you will tap and tune into, from all the rest of the wealth of information available to you, while dismissing the rest of what relates to other soul types. In other words, the calling of your intuition will be what resonates with your soul. Indeed, your soul type determines your calling and, ultimately, your path.

If you, by intuition, are a writer who falls into the Sage soul category, then only what resonates with writer types will stand out. The rest of the types are benign. The rest are for others to respond to. So many things, people, and events show up in your life, but you do not respond to or are not activated by all of them. If you have many "callings" (as I do), then many things will be activated in your life at once sometimes. That is why I'm always overwhelmed with so many things—because most of the dots in my "grid" are activated.

What is this grid I mention? As individuals, we are part of the whole, part of eternity, part of the universe, and ultimately part of the Creator. I think that the energy of the mind and body is the energy of the whole universe channeled into a person and that we have the power of the whole universe when we are in tune with it—when we mediate. The difference between human beings and the Creator is that the Creator has unlimited qualities and traits. And since we are part of the whole universe—part of the

Creator—our characteristics and traits are just a handful of those endless ones of the Creator. But for the sake of this conversation, let's say that an individual has four of these qualities or attributes: wisdom, love, justice, and creativity. That individual will channel only these attributes, which ultimately shape the "grid," so to speak, of that individual.

16

Why Do We Channel Specific Intuitive Messages and Not Others?

Microsoft Excel reads only Excel files, and Microsoft Word reads only Word files. The same concept applies to human beings, who are born with similar programs, except that these programs are the soul types discussed in chapter 15, which each person is born with.

According to Michael Teachings, who was mentioned in the previous chapter, William Shakespeare was a Scholar, JFK was a King, and Oprah Winfrey is a Sage. These famous people became who they were and are because they tuned into their soul types emanating from the many channels available to them via intuition. Those who tune in to their soul types can, however, be good or bad people. We see that in leaders, for example. When they tap into their false egos, negative things happen. That is how ruthless dictators evolve.

We are all God dismantled into pieces. And each piece (individual) has a plug that, if that individual ever goes back to God, will become "one" with God again. In our life journeys, if we purify our remote connections between God and our plugs, we will get the purity of God. Our mission, therefore, is to try to cleanse this connection as much as we can to get the best of what God has to offer relating to our soul types.

17

Follow Your Heart in That Moment

We often hear and repeat that our hearts are our guides, especially when we are stuck in a situation that needs a decision. Yet it is the best advice we can really get. "Follow your heart" does not refer to the heart organ itself or the emotions attached to the heart. It means you are to follow your voice within you, the one whispering in your ear, the one that is repeated over and over—the voice that might not be of logic or reason yet is so clear and decisive that it shows up uninvited. That voice emanates from your intuition, telling you the best aligned path you should follow and never miss.

Whatever throbs in you, especially at this moment, go along with it. Whenever your guts squeeze, that's your intuition talking with you.

Intuition Is Your Antenna Receptor

Intuition is like an antenna receptor. It channels only the frequencies available around it at a given moment. Whichever channels are available to you now are the ones you should tune in to and be with. It is a true waste if you don't do that, for they are here now and not later. When these open channels align with you, they give you a great opportunity to do anything you want. They are within you now, connecting you to this universe's intelligence. The universe will be able to provide to you now and not at any other time. That is just the nature of alignment. In other words, you cannot collect rainwater if it is not raining. You can collect rainwater only when it is raining. Here's another example: Have you ever skied during the summer or swum in a lake in Michigan in the winter? The answer is obvious yet profound. You ski when snow is available, and you swim in lakes when they are not frozen. In the same way, you can act upon what is available to you only at a specific moment. Just be aware of true alignments, be conscious of them, and just enjoy them. Living in the now is great. When you desperately seek other channels that are not available in your now, this creates a lot of challenge, and resistance occurs. This resistance will truly waste your time, your energy, and your "now." But you have to know that the desire to be with these channels is *only* because of what the ego is telling you. The ego does not get its information from intuition. It gets it from the history and accumulation of the mind, which has an agenda to feed the ego with its survival emotions, and these emotions have nothing to do with your true self and your destined path.

18

We Have All the Answers

I'm amazed by how human beings resemble computers in that they get their information from exterior sources. However, the difference is that the source of information for computers is the internet connection, which is confined and limited in nature, whereas for humans the source of information is the Creator, an unlimited and eternal source of information. In addition, the possibilities of the internet will not be realized until we connect through phone wires (ethernet) or via wireless connection. Connecting to God as a source of information is always within reach, but its degree depends on our being attuned and aligned with our intuition.

That affirms why spiritual teachers often say that answers are within us. We have the answers to all questions within ourselves. Therefore, we don't need to tap into any outside or exterior sources to get them; it's just a matter of tuning in and finding them. The New Testament is another witness to that when it says in Matthew 7:7, "Ask and it will be given to you; seek and you will find; knock and the door will be opened to you." After all, the entire universe with its abundance of resources resides in the deepest points of our souls. And that is how we have all the answers we seek in our lives.

We are governed by outside and inside forces:

- outside: emphasis on structure, logic, limits, judgment, separation from oneness, ego, insecurity
- inside: emphasis on consciousness, truth, eternity, divinity, endlessness, knowing, love, oneness, happiness, forgiveness

Intuition is a dimension within our consciousness. If we tune into it, we will immerse ourselves in a wealth of information and answers we never knew before.

If the intuition dimension is open, then one can experience the gift of healing and knowing in pursuant of the destined path.

If you tap into your intuition, you will have an unlimited source of information, abundant love, unlimited psychic ability, and pure judgment, and ultimately you will have all the answers you longed for. Intuition is indeed the highest dimension of our existence.

19

Wanting, but Not Sure What

While writing this book, I was in a void period of my life. I lost ambition in everything. I was afraid it was a sign of depression, but after reading *The Shift* by Dr. Wayne Dyer and after consulting with a spiritual friend whom I admire, I was assured that, yes, what I was going through was a void. It was the exact void I want to be in, where no ambition exists and no ego rules; in this void, there is just oneness, love, being, breathing, and creating beautiful images in my head and dwelling on them. This period was inevitable and essential for me to go through. And I knew then that I had to embrace it and go through it with full acceptance and grace.

In retrospect, my life was transforming from being ego-driven (ambition) to meaning-driven, and that is why I could not pinpoint where I was in my life. I did not know where my goals and dreams went. I felt as if I were floating in despair, with my achievements and goals dissipating in the air as if they were meaningless. It seemed as if they didn't matter—as if my life of doing, dreaming, and striving went idle. I wasn't resisting this type of feeling. I didn't know how I ended up right there, but I was there. My intuition antennae, which I had relied on for most of my life, were rusty and malfunctioning. I wrote this during that phase:

> I am writing this while I'm in this shift mode, or maybe I will stay idle. Maybe this is what we want to be when we want to have a spiritual experience. One of my friends told me that I should not force myself to do anything, and to use this time to write a daily journal. Sometimes I think that I lost my identity. I'm functioning all right, but I'm in this space of no action, no ambition, nothing pressing to work on, nothing mattering. I look at my agenda and lifetime goals I have written and always referred to and worked at, and I don't see a need to do any of it.
>
> I don't know how the next part of my life is going to be or when it will unfold, but I'm embracing and enjoying what I'm going through right now, and I know that it is a platform for my new evolvement in my destined path. I just have to remember to be kind to myself and be patient even if I'm confused about what I want, until my intuition kicks in.

20

Listen to the Voices of Angels, Not to the Voices of Demons

Maybe it's drastic to call voices demons and angels, but the point is obvious: in order to follow your heart, and ultimately your path, you need to listen to what aligns you with it and not what derails you from it.

These voices have two sources; one is inside of you, and one is outside of you. The source inside of you is inside your head and your mind, talking to you all the time. The outside source is that of the voices of the people around you, what you perceive, and what you hear. Always acquaint yourself with and be in the company of individuals who affirm your positive thinking and believe in you (sometimes even more than you believe in yourself). These people were sent to your path to affirm your alignment with your intuition and path. On the other hand, individuals who doubt you, always put you down, exhaust you, make you feel bad about yourself, and always ask you, "Oh, but how you are going to accomplish that?" were sent to your path to derail you. Those people can love you but have so much fear and limitation that they mirror themselves to you. The decision about whom to listen to, whom to accompany, and who is right will always be yours. These people are indeed the ones who believe in you and have no doubt whatsoever that you are going to be whoever you want to be and accomplish whatever you want to accomplish without buts, hows, and ohs.

Imagine yourself as a machine. The fuel is the people who come into your life. If you have a machine that requires oil to operate, you will use oil. You will not use any other form of fuel; that will not work. That is exactly why you should be with the people who will give you fuel for your journey. Other types of energy will not *ever* work for you.

21

Why Do We Say Some People Are More Loving than Others?

Having intuition is the nature of all human beings—no exceptions. If you have a mother, then ultimately you have a connection to the Source via the umbilical cord remnant behind the belly button where the plug of the antenna of intuition resides.

In the context of intuition, people full of love are those whose pure intuition has been tapped into. This means love resides in all of us, even in the most vicious people. But why don't some people give love or pursue acts of love? This subject is very serious, complicated, and multifaceted. In the context of intuition, these types of people have not tapped into the purity—I repeat, the purity—of their intuitive selves, which is an abundant source of love.

But the important question here is, What makes people tap into love more than others, or not at all? The following facets in life make us more or less conscious of love:

- family influence; the way we are brought up
- level of education
- confidence that we have love
- focused attention
- our spiritual journeys
- trust in our intuition
- feelings of validation and being heard
- feelings of worthiness
- feelings of being loved and being capable of giving love

The degree of love imbedded in our intuition and ultimately in our actions is a reflection of what we have acquired at a given point in our lives. And this is exactly why we tap into what we resonate with, which could be more of love, more of evil, or more of something in between. What I tap into is different from what you tap into, even though we share the same source.

22

How Letting Go Relates to Letting God

When you let go, you tell your body and soul to relax. Immediately after, a physical and spiritual opening will be created, directly connecting you to your pure intuition—to God and His abundance and creation. Then, and only then, you don't need to do anything; you may let go and let God do the work.

Since God creates without effort, and since creativity is effortless, letting go means letting the abundant and creative work of God be accessible and displayed without interfering. This means that doing nothing will allow God to do His work. When we interfere, the channeling of God's work will be offset and will not manifest when we tap into His source. Therefore, we should not block it or challenge it. Just let it be. Just let go and let God, so to speak.

If we let go and be connected to God, only then will every possible path be possible to attain.

23

How to Activate Your Intuition

This is how you activate your intuition:

- when you open yourself to unlimited possibilities;
- when you trust in yourself and do not doubt yourself;
- when you open your heart to everything you encounter;
- when you consciously listen to the voices residing within and inside of you;
- when you meditate and dive deep within yourself;
- when you listen to silence and experience nature; and
- when you do what you love, and be in the moment of giving without asking in return,

then and only then do you open yourself, connect it to the Source, tap into its wealth by being in the moment, and inevitably activate your intuition. So, basically you tap into intuition by listening in not out. These activities make you closer to your Creator and subsequently to the abundant wealth of information it possesses.

24

Can Intuitions Collide?

If you are true to your intuition and the other person is true to his or her intuition, then there is no way they will collide. Why? Because they originate from the same source, which is integrated, cohesive, comprehensive, and never in conflict with itself. Therefore, these intuitions will support and complete each other rather than collide.

25

Coincidences? I Don't Think So

In the context of this book's discussion, coincidence, or synchrodestiny, should be called "alignment of two separate intuitions." When different intuitions get the same information from the Source at a certain time, they have the same intention. And when they act upon it, they align in action. And that is how coincidences happen. These two intuitions happen to be of the same frequency; they tune into each other, they synchronize and get the same message from the universe, and, in turn, they display the same outcome.

Explaining it from a different perspective, Dr. Deepak Chopra, an author, alternative medicine advocate, and prominent figure in the New Age movement, discussed synchrodestiny in his book *Meta Human* (2019). He said that synchrodestinies are orchestrated in a nonlocal domain. They happen simultaneously where no space or time exists. They happen in a higher dimension of reality—in a cosmic consciousness. An intention happens, and as a result of syncrodestiny, one will be made conscious of the purpose of one's life, which is one's karma, or the calling of one's life.

But why are synchrodestinies important when talking about intuition? As Dr. Chopra explains in *The Spontaneous Fulfillment of Desire* (2004), as we become more aware of coincidences and their meaning, we begin to connect more with the infinite possibilities that reside in our intuition in the first place. This is when we achieve the fulfillment of our desires, which gives us the ultimate feeling of happiness and satisfaction.

26

The Power of Family Prayers

What happens if a family meditates on one thought of healing for the sake of one of their own, or for a specific intended wish to come true? Let's first start exploring the idea of the law of attraction, which itself is a big subject. It basically suggests that a person can attract whatever he or she visualizes and thinks of. What if this individual law of attraction for the same thought gets multiplied by a beautiful number? What if eight or eighteen people intend the same thought, for example? And what if these people are from the same family? What would happen? You definitely know the answer.

Plenty of research affirms that powerful thoughts create energies with vibrations that can attract their equivalents from the universe in its totality. This fascinated me, and I knew there must be a convincing rationale behind it. It took me a while until I got my hands on the one-mind concept introduced by physician and author Dr. Larry Dossey in his book *One Mind*. He refers to one particular piece of research conducted by psychophysiologist Dr.

Jeanne Achterberg (and published in 2005), in which she recruited eleven healers. Dr. Achterberg concluded from MRI scans of the subjects that compassionate healing intentions, or what she called "distant Intentionality," in the form of prayers, energy, and good intentions, cause measurable physical effects on remote recipients and that the connection between the healers and recipients is vital during the process of healing—contrary to what most of the world thinks about the fact that the mind is isolated to the brain itself. Dr. Dossey suggests that healing results from the encounter of the one-mind experience. That is why praying together intensely on one thought has a significant outcome based on the notion of "one mind." In fact, according to Marriam-Webster Dictionary, *heal* is derived from a Middle English *helen*, from Old English *hǣlan*; akin to Old High German *heilen* to heal, Old English *hāl* whole.

Let's take this notion even further. What if those eight or eighteen individuals who are sending prayers and healing energies are members of the same family? We know that a blood-related family maintains quite a bit of the same fabric and DNA of the umbilicus in each one of them as given from the mothers' umbilical cords. And when siblings in particular, for example, focus on one deep thought in a meditation or prayer in unison, the collective thoughts are magnified as one powerful, pure vibrational energy that will attract their likes from the universe as they synchronize with the same channeling of God's information. That is why great things would happen in such a case. While you might argue that there is no research supporting that notion, there is, however, plenty of evidence that they happen every day and everywhere.

The power of positive energy and thoughts doesn't know boundaries; nor is it affected by distances. That energy is part of the cosmic consciousness, which is defined by psychiatrist Richard Maurice Bucke as a form of higher consciousness than that which is possessed by the ordinary man, in which space and

Unveiling the Physical Source of Intuition

time don't exist, especially when it comes to energy. Therefore, the intensity and effect of positive energy are equally effective whether energy is intended remotely or nearby. Having said that, if positive thoughts and intense prayers get bigger and multiply in magnitude, then their effectiveness is multiplied and intensified proportionally wherever they happen in this universe.

27

The Mystery of Identical Twins Resolved

It's not a miracle or a mystery that identical twins have the same thoughts and take the same actions. It actually confirms my theory about the umbilicus (the umbilical cord remnant) being the physical place of intuition. Twins share 100 percent of the same DNA of the umbilical cord passed from their mother's one placenta; thus, they have the same plug, and ultimately, they have the same identical connection to the Source and the same flow of information at a given time. As mentioned earlier, the source of information resides where God left us on earth, which is the umbilical cord remnant, and since the umbilical cords are from the same placenta, everything is identical. That's it. They think, behave, and respond in the same ways. Mystery solved. And there is no other explanation except this simple one.

28

How Human Beings Are Connected to Each Other

The realization that the special connection I have with specific people exists merely because we are from the same spiritual soul type fascinates me. And in my case, my spiritual guide is of the Teacher type.

As you know, there are seven spiritual guides: Gatekeeper, Teacher, Protector, Runner, Helper, Warrior, and Joy. They are spiritual beings who have had human experiences and have come back again to guide human beings.

I know that I am visited by the Teacher guide because writing and spiritual development are coming to me through my connection to God—my intuition. And that is why, for example, Dr. Wayne W. Dyer and other writers are connected to me and I'm connected to them. We all share the same Teacher guide type. This God-given and inherited entity will keep us aligned in a path toward our destinies. That is why these types of individuals who came before me keep showing up in my life.

29

Worry, Fear, and Intuition

Why do we like to worry instead of letting go? Because worry is a form of thinking that is considered the activity within the brain that most occupies it. But why is this so important to us?

Human beings subconsciously trust the mind more than anything in the world. We think the mind is the most sacred, superior phenomena we ever possess, and that if we follow its logic, the outcome will be the right one. But what does this have to do with our obsession with worrying? We don't trust storing our "eager thoughts about our issues (our worries)" somewhere other than in this mind. So we like to keep the worries in our minds in an effort to control them and not let them slip away. We don't want to store them anywhere else in our realms or entities. We think that the best way to marinate upon them and solve them is to store and control them in our minds. We trust only our own energy fields. If we empty our brains of these worries, we feel as if we are not loyal to the causes of our issues or worries. We like to juggle them in the different chambers of our minds, searching for logic, solutions, manifestation, and comfort. We don't trust that they might be, in fact, mostly fabrications of the mind itself. But what is the alternative? How about we just let go of them? Don't worry; they will be handled by the Source and the events and dynamics of the universe. As you know everything has an end to it.

Why don't we let go of worry? When we think about an issue, our brain does not calculate the fact that all other dynamics of the universe are in a constant state of change and molding. The mind does not include this when it tries to solve an issue. And when an issue gets solved on its own, we call it either a miracle or good luck. It is neither. This occurs because the dynamics of the universe have aligned themselves in such a way that the issue is taken care of. Every second in this life is unique. It calibrates the residue of the previous one and subsequently becomes the base for the next one.

Now that we have talked about worry, let's talk about fear. But first, what is the difference between worry and fear? Worry is shallow and weak, yet fear is more powerful.

While listening in my car to an audiobook *How to Get What You Really, Really, Really, Really Want,* by Dr. Wayne W. Dyer (Narrator, Author) and Deepak Chopra MD (Narrator, Author), about knowing versus belief, my thoughts were dominated by a fearful thought I had that day about a work situation. I feared I had made a mistake. Then it hit me like lightning: I knew why I had that fear. The issue at work was in an area that was out of my knowing, away from my path, and distant from my passion. My take is that fear does not exist in the world of one's intuitive path because knowing has no fear. When there is knowing, fear dissipates. That is why I believe that fearless people work from their guts—from their intuition, a place of no fear. The knowing part, while I was following my intuition, was always overshadowed by the fear of being away from it and lacking it (knowing), and that is what I was doing.

30

Food Craving and Intuition

Are food cravings and intuition connected? I believe so. Just like so many of you, I tend to crave specific kinds of food or drink. This tendency might last a day, a week, or even months. I have always nourished my cravings and never denied them. And in all honesty, I have never felt guilty about eating however much I have wanted of what I have been craving. But why is this lack of guilt so powerful?

One day while writing this book, I was on my way to work and thinking about what to cook that day. I didn't have to think twice. It would, of course, bake the red potato fries I had been eating for three days in a row. It hit me like a flash that the cause of my craving was deep in my intuition. How is that possible—and why? As we know, everything in this universe has an energy field, including our intuition, as discussed in chapter 1. When its energy field gets derailed or unbalanced, it searches for a different one that will balance it and keep it on track. So when I was craving the potatoes, this was because my intuition was in search of energy to balance it. The solution was indeed the potatoes. But when do we know when to stop? And how do we know that it is getting out of hand? We have to tune in deep inside and determine whether a craving is healthy or not. We have to listen to the deeper messages within ourselves.

Intuition is our default apparatus—our own autopilot that will act and decide—or, in other words, will have all the action and decision ready when there is no logical or thoughtful decision. In some religions and cultures, when someone is hesitant to make a decision, especially when both extremes are weighted equally, oftentimes the individual is guided in decision-making by a gut feeling generated after a special prayer. Alternatively, on a far less logical basis, an individual can get inspiration from whatever script his or her eyes fall on after randomly opening a holy book. Being so desperate for a decision is not healthy. I have always believed in what Lao Tzu said in the *Tao Te Ching,* as I mentioned in chapter 13: "Do you have the patience to wait till your mud settles and the water is clear? Can you remain unmoving till the right action arises by itself?"

31

The Link between Disease and Intuition

> When the drop of water rejoins the ocean it has all the powers of its source.
>
> —Dr. Wayne Dyer

In a blog post titled "There Is a Solution", accessed April 21, 2019, https://www.drwaynedyer.com/blog/there-is-a-solution, Dr. Wayne Dyer writes, "Like a drop of water separated from its source the little mind is unable to create and sustain life. When the drop of water rejoins the ocean it has all the powers of its source. The drop of water separate from its source symbolizes our ego-self when we are separated from our source of omnipotent power."

Adapting the same metaphor, the human body is a perfect entity and works at its best when all its organs and its cells are connected in a cohesive and balanced way, immersed in one energy field that is plugged to the remnant of the umbilical cord. But when some cells derail (or get out of the "orderly wholeness," as I call it, which they were in before)—when human cells forget their identities and fall out of their rhythms—they no longer get the same information the rest of the cells are getting from the Creator via the umbilical cord remnants. They don't properly get access to the source of information and instructions from the brain (their main supplier). They start to behave irrationally and not in parallel with their functions. This is obviously because they disconnect from the source of information.

The medical world, and Western medicine in particular, has a different take. But I think that when human cells forget who they are—their identities—they don't properly get command signal impulses from their main supplier. This disconnect or void makes the human cells process information in a totally different way than normal. Take the case of cancer, for example. Cancer causes abnormal cell growth that cannot be contained—an erratic growth with no specific path. Sometimes this disconnect takes a different path, and a cell forgets that certain other cells are its own. This is the case in autoimmune diseases, such as arthritis, where the immune system mistakes part of the body, such as the joints, as foreign, and it releases protein called autoantibodies that attack healthy cells.

The way I like to describe the disconnectedness of the cells in diseases is that it is just like a grid of hundreds of Christmas lights. When one of the lights loses its function, and ultimately its connection to the whole grid, it not only turns off but also disrupts the entire grid. The wellness of just one is the foundation to the wellness of a whole.

The body functions and thrives on being one collective mass of energy, which happens only when its cells and organs are totally connected and tuned into their one source of intuition. That is where healing can tag along and reverse the situation, as explained in chapter 11.

32

Revenge, Anger, Hate, and Intuition

The emotions listed in the title of this chapter have one thing in common: they are all negative energies that can invade our mental realms and cause harm to us and others. They are activated in us by one of two forces: derailment from the intuitive self and submission to the calls of negative emotions.

I created an equation pattern inspired by Eckhart Tolle's *The Power of Now*, in which I inserted these negative emotions. Then, in contrast to it, I created a pattern of positive emotions.

> Negative Emotions (identify with mind) = pain (emotional) = unconscious spirituality = hatred = self-pity = guilt = grief = rage = anger = revenge = fear = shame = jealousy = disappointment = all other negative emotions

> Positive Emotions (identify with no mind) = pure consciousness = no thinking = creativity =

being = compassion = love, peace, and joy (from beyond the mind) = gratitude = forgiveness = unmanifested = presence = what is = deathless = formless = eternal = now

In psychology, emotions are altered by desires. As Buddha said, that pain or suffering arises through desire or craving, and to be free from pain, we need to cut the bonds of desire. Desire can be either positive or negative, such as the desire for revenge, desire for anger, desire for hate, and so on. These desires, in turn, mold our emotions.

Acting on negative emotions, if they were the cause of derailments, will not resolve them. The world would have been structured differently if humans were intended to act upon these negative feelings. Therefore, both tuning into our pure calling and intuition without falling into the trap of derailing, in addition to living in a desireless stage and practicing mindfulness (keeping the mind empty) ultimately will take you right on your path.

33

Intuition Is to Blame for Procrastination After All

Procrastination has always bothered me, especially when I'm trying to finish a task at work yet I'm reluctant to do it or even hate doing it. While writing this book, I realized why—and why I'm fully devoted to and passionate about tasks at certain times but not at others. Sometimes I do a task perfectly and efficiently, and when I finish it, I feel great. And while I'm doing it, it makes me feel so in the moment (the right moment, to be exact) that I feel aligned with something greater than me. I feel vibration of a different high frequency, and the task is done in total perfection. At a different time, this task would have taken me five times the time needed to finish it, it wouldn't have been as perfect, and I wouldn't have been that happy performing it. How do I complete my tasks perfectly and efficiently? I channel energy. I unconsciously wait for the moment when my antenna of my intuition plug aligns with the pure abundant Source—when all things in the universe come together to get a given task done at the perfect time and in the best way it's ever been done.

We procrastinate because our minds try to find the right time to do a task. In other words, our minds want to find their best niches in the universe. It has nothing to do with being lazy, postponing a task, or having no time to do something. The right time to do something—isn't that what we discussed in chapter 13? I am so happy to have realized this fact. It makes me feel so good. Now I can just trust my intuition, which will guide me to the best times to do different tasks and to perform them to the fullest, and those times in which an abundance of resources is available for them to be done flawlessly, perfectly, and efficiently. So how do you accomplish your to-do list effortlessly while enjoying the process?

I did not want to continue doing things and hating them. I am spiritual, and I need to go with the flow of how I feel in the moment—the flow of my intuition, waiting for the signal—but these to-dos are an important part of my life. I learned there come times when I do things effortlessly, effectively, willingly, and with so much joy. I was fascinated by this. I added things to my to-do list and just waited for "the moment" to call me to do one of them. I wondered why this happened. These moments just come to me; it is as if the universe decides when to do things, not me. It seems that the universe has the best control of my schedule.

After writing this chapter, I started to accomplish my tasks in all aspects of my life, including at work, one by one, without feeling pressured or obligated. Of course, this does not work 100 percent of the time, since there are must-do things in our daily lives that we cannot deny or postpone—at least not yet.

I can wait until the "naturally grass-fed" cows come home to feel that I really want to do something. But it is only up to the flow of intuition whether this will happen or not.

Human beings live with the flow of the universe—what it's providing at any moment without any resistance or suffering. For example, many communities focus their diets on seasonal fruits and vegetables. This is similar to why we need to do a specific task at a specific time and not others—because that time is "seasonal" too. It's available to us—harvested from our intuition—now and not later.

Seasonal fruits and vegetables are fresher and tastier than those harvested out of season. They are environmentally friendly. They have more nutrients if they are picked when naturally ripened and harvested at the right time. They are also less expensive because they are sourced from non-local areas of various climates. As Kelly LeVeque, a certified holistic health coach, discusses in her article "10 Reasons to Eat What's in Season", accessed on November 19, 2019, www.mindbodygreen.com, eating seasonal food is supportive to our seasonal needs, which facilitate our bodies' natural healing process. For example, eating apples in the fall helps the body cool down before winter, and eating watermelon in the summer helps us cool down and stay hydrated. But the most fascinating reason LeVeque discussed was that tuning with nature's rhythm makes us live in balance with our surroundings instead of in conflict with them and allows us to embrace natural rhythms of things to simplify life, among other things.

I have always struggled to stay on course—meaning not scattered here and there, doing so many different things and trying so hard to finish them. Now I know why. You might have guessed it already. In fact, I have not just one of the soul types we talked about in previous chapters, but rather plenty of them. I was given lots of them when my form was created. That multifold divine fabric is, in fact, the reason why nothing in the human dimension gets accomplished unless I can get the support and help of others.

34

Creativity and Intuition

When you work and perform from the deepest points of inspiration in you (your creative essence), you are fully connected to your Creator through your plug of intuition and will have access to the unlimited sources of the Creator's qualities and characteristics. That is why you become best at what inspires you. It is the perfection of the Creator shown through you.

Letting Go and Creativity

As I touched on in chapter 22, when you let go and do nothing, you destroy all boundaries around you. You ignite the Creator in you to be free and to do what it has eternally done, which is create. That is how you let God, in you, create. And that is how it will become *you* creating to show. For you to be creative, you have to do one thing: just let go of everything. It is effortless. Indeed, the creative process is effortless. When you let go 100 percent indefinitely and endlessly, your creation will be that of the Creator. That is why creative people are more intuitive than others.

35

How Intuition Shaped History

So many critical decisions made by legends and leaders throughout different civilizations and historic periods, including Julius Caesar, Alexander the Great, and Napoleon Bonaparte, were made based on nothing more than intuition. But what type of intuition was it? The ordinary, raw intuition I have been talking about in this book, or a different type? Dr. William Duggan, an associate professor at Colombia Business School and author of *Napoleon's Glance: The Secret of Strategy,* ponders that question in one of his courses, Napoleon's Glance. According to Dr. Duggan, in 1832, the book *On War* by Carl Von Clausewitz revealed that the secret to the genius and success of Napoleon, who won more battles than any general in recorded history, was the Napoleon glance, or what he called *"Coup D'Oeil"* (which means "glance" in French). It is described as a sudden insight when a quick decision needs to be made that guides one to a course of action based on the knowledge one has acquired from past experiences. Today this is called *strategic intuition*, and it has spread to other fields, such as business and art. Duggan further explains in his course outline that while ordinary intuition is a feeling, strategic intuition is based on real knowledge and experiences that come in a flash from similar situations, which, as psychologist Gary Klein suggested, are stored in memories to suit a specific situation. Then the "big a-has," as he describes, will manifest into decisions, as also is the case in innovation. Napoleon's glance was also the reason behind the success of other strategies, such as how Joan of Arc saved France from England and how Picasso became the most famous artist of the twentieth century.

None of these decisions of such great leaders were made based on logic, mathematics, reason, analysis, or a premeditated thought. They were all pure intuition, strongly heartfelt by these leaders. Yet look at how they changed the paths of these civilizations and, ultimately, the world we live in—right or wrong.

Now that the world is becoming more evolved regarding spirituality, you can already see how humans are seriously tapping into their spirituality to shape the many facets of lives. My take is that in the future, lots of uncertainties are going to be similarly decided based on intuition as we lean more in support of being more in tune with our spirituality.

36

Now What?

Now that we know what intuition is and how we are plugged into the source of abundant information from the Creator, what is next—and why is this finding important, anyway?

If you align yourself consciously with your intuition, you will most likely make the best decisions of your life—those that will always make your journey meaningful—and you will stay true to your path. Ultimately this process will align your spiritual growth to its ultimate, highest destined path meant to be yours. After all, the only treasure we were given since our birth is our connection to this universe's true and abundant information.

37

Intuition: Continuity and Living in the Now

Intuition is the vibe that decides your *now*—from one second to the next, and on to the rest. Your life is led by your intuitionality, as I call it. If every moment you live in is guided by your intuition and by what is best for that moment, then this will enhance and enrich your living in the now at its best. What can best guide you other than intuition itself? In other words, if you follow your intuition—your heart—every moment, you need not fear anything; you are guided by the Source—your Creator.

Therefore, you cannot live in the now without letting your intuition be the center of your action, taking command. As a matter of fact, that is why so many people cannot live in the now no matter how hard they try—because, yes, they become conscious, but the intuition is missing. They don't or cannot tap into it. So "living in the now" becomes a phrase that is replaced, as they practice in futility.

38
Happiness in Everything Is Connected to the Creator

When you are in oneness with the Creator, you feel happy, even if the happiness stems from you indulging in eating a piece of chocolate. Your mind does not work when you are connecting to the Creator and indulging. You become part of the unconditional love, where no worries, judgments, or hate resides. That is why it is hard to mix the mind/logic with eating great food. While logic tells you to eat reasonably, the subconscious "without mind" tells you to connect to the magnificent feeling of happiness.

39

Linking Religions and Faiths Intuitionally

I promised myself not to get into a discussion about religion (not only in this book, but in all of my future books). However, it's very hard to dismiss the beautiful fact that what is common in all faiths and religions in this universe is that all of them simply preach that one is to follow one's heart. After reading this book, you know that what's in the heart is what the Creator and the universe are telling you to follow.

40

How Intuitive Are You?

I would love to hear about what you all have to say after reading this book. You may share your ideas and thoughts on my website, www.buthaynataha.com. By doing so, you will be helping me write the second edition of this book, which will contain even more intriguing stories of yours.

Conclusion

The revolutionary finding about the physical source of intuition presented in this book is going to open lots of other intriguing findings about our source or nonsource of creation, and more value and insight about intuition itself.

My final thought summing up intuition is this: Intuition comes from an unlimited field of information. It is raw, and it is the best treasure you have if you tap into it. It is a gift from the Creator, given to you to use or not use. It can optimize and "utopialize" your path, your purpose, your identity, your type, and, ultimately, your connection to this universe and to everything and everyone in it.

My question to you is, How much has reading this book affected you or changed how you think about intuition in your life?

I'm really wondering whether you feel the same way about intuition or your previous experiences with it after reading this book. I'm sure that some of you are thinking, "Yes, these findings are known to me, but I have never tapped into them." It is ironic to say it this way, isn't it?

I know why I have always been inspired by and connected to the stories of so many celebrities, no matter what talents they possess or whether I like their talents or not. The reason for this is because they have no doubt they want to be what they already became. They follow who they are. They follow their intuition. They tap into their soul types in a positive manner. They rarely listen to the negative criticism all around them.

I truly believe that if we deny our gifts via our intuition, we become traitors to God's purpose given to us on earth. Doing so would be to deny ourselves the greatest treasure given to us through our intuition since our existence on this earth.